Jamie Bell

# Praise Him!
# Praise Him!

by Jennie Davis
illustrated by
Kathryn Hutton

Published by The Dandelion House
A Division of The Child's World

Distributed by Scripture Press Publications, Wheaton, Illinois 60187.

**Library of Congress Cataloging in Publication Data**

Davis, Jennie.
  Praise Him! Praise Him!

  Summary: A little girl thanks Jesus for the beauty,
enjoyment, and love He provides.
    1. Children—Prayer-books and devotions—English.
[1. Prayer books and devotions.   2. Gratitude]
  I.  Hutton, Kathryn, ill.   II. Title.
BT202.M557              242'.62              82-7238
  ISBN 0-89693-208-7                          AACR2

Published by The Dandelion House, A Division of The Child's World, Inc.

1 2 3 4 5 6 7 8 9 10 11 12 R  89 88 87 86 85 84 83 82

*Let all the children praise Him, Jesus our Lord!*

For Your love,
O Lord,
my praises I bring.

I praise You,
Lord Jesus,
for everything.

For sunshine and flowers,
for big oak trees,

for butterflies

and honey bees,

for baby robins
too small to sing—
I praise You, Lord Jesus,
for everything.

For rain and ducklings,
for frisky frogs,

9

for turtles

and fish

and polliwogs,

for fun on a see-saw,
a slide, a swing—
I thank You, Lord Jesus,
for everything.

I praise You, Lord,
for each new day.
I praise You for friends
who come to play.

For summer

and fall,

for winter

and spring,

I praise You, Lord Jesus,
for everything.

I thank You, Lord,
for a place to sleep,

warm clothes to wear,

and food to eat.

I praise You, Lord,
for giving to me. . .
my very special family. . .

Grandma and Grandpa,

Mom and Dad,

my sister, Anne,

and my brother, Chad.

And I praise You, too,
for my church family. . .

for those who show
Your love to me.

And as I worship
on this Your day,
when church bells ring
and choirs sing. . .

29

I praise You, Lord,
for everything.

# All the Children Praise Him

S. B. D.

STELLA B. DALEBURN

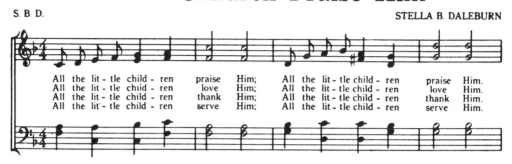

All the lit - tle child - ren praise Him; All the lit - tle child - ren praise Him.
All the lit - tle child - ren love Him; All the lit - tle child - ren love Him.
All the lit - tle child - ren thank Him; All the lit - tle child - ren thank Him.
All the lit'- tle child - ren serve Him; All the lit - tle child - ren serve Him.

Praise Him, praise Him, praise Him, praise Him, Je - sus, God's dear Son.
Love Him, love Him, love Him, love Him, Je - sus first loved us.
Thank Him, thank Him, thank Him, thank Him; He is good to all.
Serve Him, serve Him, serve Him, serve Him; Je - sus is our King.

*ACTION: Clap hands with singing of "praise Him".*
*Hold arms in embrace with singing of "love Him".*
*Bow Heads with singing of "thank Him".*
*Extend hands with singing of "serve Him".*